How adults like to learn

A NIACE briefing on learning and skills development outside of the workplace

Taken from the NIACE Survey on Adult Participation in Learning 2008

Fiona Aldridge and Alan Tuckett

EUROPEAN UNION
European Social Fund

Local Government Association

promoting adult learning

Published by the National Institute of Adult Continuing Education (England and Wales)

21 De Montfort Street
Leicester LE1 7GE
Company registration no. 2603322
Charity registration no. 1002775

NIACE, the national organisation for adult learning, has a broad remit to promote lifelong learning opportunities for adults. NIACE works to develop increased participation in education and training, particularly for those who do not have easy access because of barriers of class, gender, age, race, language and culture, learning difficulties and disabilities, or insufficient financial resources.

NIACE's website on the internet is **http://www.niace.org.uk**

Cataloguing in Publication Data
A CIP record of this title is available from the British Library

ISBN 978 1 86201 363 6

EUROPEAN UNION
European Social Fund

The production of this publication has been part-funded through the European Social Fund. The European Social Fund is a European Union initiative that supports activities to extend employment opportunities and develop a skilled workforce.

Contents

Acknowledgements

We are grateful for the support of the European Social Fund and the Local Government Association in the funding of this work; of our colleagues at RSGB who conducted the research; and of our colleagues at NIACE in the production of this report.

Introduction

In January the Secretary of State for Innovation, Universities and Skills launched a major consultation on the role of informal learning in public life in England.[1] In part, the consultation seeks to map the richness of self-organised learning, whether through the activities of allotment societies, gardening clubs, reading groups or through the more organised activities of local universities of the third age. It was interested, too, in how libraries, museums and galleries, football clubs and ramblers' groups help support their users' learning. It was interested, too, in the role new technologies play in supporting adult learning – looking for evidence of how patients equip themselves more effectively in discussions with their doctors on the implications for treatment of medical conditions, or how people explore the genealogy of their families. One clear issue that will arise for government as a result of the consultation is the appropriate relationship between more structured learning, such as that offered in adult education classes, like those organised by the Workers' Educational Association and local education authorities, and this wealth of informal learning. How best can government support self-organised activity, and what is the role of public provision for learning for personal and community development? These are key questions at a time when public funded enrolments by adults have fallen by more than 1,400,000 in two years,[2] and when participation in any sort of learning has fallen significantly.[3]

To help to inform the consultation, NIACE decided to add questions to its annual adult participation in learning survey of 5,000 adults in the UK to find out how adults like to learn new things. The additional questions explore which of ten forms of learning and skills acquisition adults find useful for learning outside work, and builds on earlier NIACE surveys of preferred learning style at work.[4] The questions draw on the distinction developed by Alan Felstead and his colleagues in the ESRC study on workplace learning between learning as 'participation' and learning as 'acquisition'.[5] This distinguishes between learning gained informally, through discussion and reflection and learning gained through structured activities where the learning goal is explicit. Each time NIACE has undertaken the survey of adults in employment (in 2004, 2006 and 2007), workers have expressed clear preferences for learning on the job, through being shown by peer groups or managers how to do activities or tasks. Of the ten forms of learning and skills development explored with workers, courses and structured training activities have come consistently

1   DIUS (2008) *Informal Adult Learning – Shaping the Way Ahead*, available at www.adultlearningconsultation.org.uk (accessed 24 April 2008).
2   LSC (2007) *Further Education, Work Based Learning, Train to Gain and Adult and Community Learning – Learner Numbers in England 2006/07*, available at http://readingroom.lsc.gov.uk/lsc/National/nat-ilrsfr 14-dec07.pdf (accessed 24 April 2008).
3   Aldridge, F. and Tuckett A. (2008) *Counting the Cost: The NIACE Survey on Adult Participation in Learning 2008*, NIACE: Leicester.
4   Aldridge, F. and Tuckett A. (2007) *Practice makes perfect: A NIACE briefing on learning at work: Taken from the 2007 NIACE survey on adult participation in learning*, NIACE: Leicester.
5   See www.learningaswork.cf.ac.uk.

fourth. The implications of this are clear – effective strategies to increase skills and knowledge levels in the UK workforce need to secure a culture of informal learning alongside more structured qualifications bearing learning programmes if employees are to have maximum benefit.

The current study confirms the importance of informal modes of learning for the learning that adults undertake outside work, and that they prefer learning as participation to learning as acquisition, though outside work learners have a more eclectic enthusiasm for learning, finding a wider variety of strategies useful than learners at work (Table 1). The findings highlight the importance and timeliness of the policy focus on informal learning, but also make clear that for a majority of adults learning through attendance at courses remains of importance. For the informal learning consultation this is an important conclusion – suggesting that a blend of publicly offered classes and informal provision is the right mix for community based learning.

However, there are significant differences from the earlier studies of workers (Table 2). The regular undertaking of a task was seen as far more useful as a way of learning at work than for learning outside work. By contrast, reading books, manuals and magazines, and using the Internet were all of greater significance outside work – perhaps a finding of some importance during this National Year of Reading.[6] There is a sharp difference between work and learning outside work for different socio-economic groups, as well. Outside work, for social class C2 courses were reported as the most helpful of all the options for learning as acquisition, though only a minority of socio-economic group DE found any of the more formal routes to learning useful (Table 6).

Current and recent learners show greater confidence in the usefulness of all ten forms of learning than people who say they have done no learning since leaving school (Table 3). What is surprising perhaps, is that those people who say they have done no learning since school, and those who have no plans to take up learning in the next three years retain relatively high levels of confidence in the helpfulness of a range of forms of learning new skills. This may suggest that they do not identify their strategies for developing knowledge and skills as 'learning', or that whilst they do not anticipate the need to develop knowledge or skills, they are confident that they would have the tools to hand should they do so.

There are significant age differences reported in the survey (Table 8). It is perhaps to be expected that younger people are more at ease with the Internet, expected, too, that the perceived helpfulness of all forms of learning decline with age. The report makes clear, though, that learning through courses and through trial and error are of particular importance to people in their thirties. And work does it seem help with learning. Both full-time and part-time workers, and unemployed people report finding more forms of learning helpful than those outside the labour market, or retired (Table 7). This highlights in a fresh way a particular challenge facing government in seeking 80 per cent participation rates in the labour market, since people currently neither in work nor seeking work combine having lower levels of skill than the rest of the population and as reported here, less confidence in using different strategies for learning new things.

---

6   www.yearofreading.co.uk

Technical notes

In 2004, 2006 and 2007, NIACE worked alongside a team of researchers, now at Cardiff University, the Institute of Education in London and the University of Southampton to devise a module of questions on learning at work for insertion into its Adult Participation in Learning survey.

As part of the 2008 survey, a key question from this module was adapted to explore learning and skills development outside of the workplace. This survey, undertaken for NIACE, by RSGB, interviewed a weighted sample of 4,932 adults, aged 17 and over, in the UK in the period 20 February to 29 March 2008.

The survey includes a range of questions on adult participation in learning, although this report is mainly concerned with the findings from the following question on learning and skills development outside of the workplace. Additional reports will be published on the full range of data throughout the year.

"Thinking about any learning or skills development that you have undertaken outside of work, please tell me to what extent each one of the following activities has been most effective in developing your knowledge or skills. So, firstly…

… Undertaking an activity on a regular basis
… Being shown by others how to do activities or tasks
… Watching and listening to others while they carry out activities
… Reflecting on your performance
… Using trial and error
… Using the Internet
… Reading books, manuals and magazines
… Using skills and abilities acquired elsewhere
… Drawing on the knowledge and skills you picked up while studying for a qualification
… Training courses paid for by your employer or yourself

01: A great deal of help
02: Quite a lot of help
03: Of some help
04: A little help
05: Of no help at all
06: Don't know

Throughout this report percentages are rounded to the nearest whole number. Owing to this, and sensitivities introduced by weighting, some categories in the following tables may sum to slightly more than or less than 100 per cent. Further, any percentages calculated on small bases should be treated with caution as they may be subject to wide margins of sampling error. Tables are percentaged vertically unless otherwise specified. In tables, * indicates less than 0.5 per cent but greater than zero, and − indicates zero. NSR indicates not separately recorded and NA indicates not asked.

Developing knowledge and skills outside of work

In 2004, 2006 and 2007, respondents in employment were asked to identify activities that they considered to have been most useful in helping them to learn to do their job better. The survey found that activities associated with the workplace were of more help in raising performance then learning by acquisition (typified by training courses and qualifications).

As part of the 2008 survey, this question was adapted to explore whether the same pattern emerged in relation to learning undertaken outside of work (see Table 1). The survey found that adults consider the most effective means of developing knowledge and skills outside of the workplace to include being shown how to do tasks and activities by other people (64 per cent), undertaking an activity on a regular basis (60 per cent), watching and listening to others while they carry out activities (57 per cent) and reading books, manuals and magazines (57 per cent).

Just over one half of respondents think that attending training courses (53 per cent), drawing on skills picked up while studying for a qualification (53 per cent), and using skills and abilities acquired elsewhere (52 per cent) are very or quite helpful in developing knowledge and skills outside of the workplace. Slightly fewer find reflecting on performance (49 per cent) or using trial and error (46 per cent) to be a helpful approach.

One-quarter of respondents report finding the Internet of little or no help at all in developing their skills and knowledge.

Table 1: Forms of learning and skills development outside of work, 2008

	Very or quite helpful %	Of some help %	Of little or no help %	Don't know %
Learning as acquisition				
Reading books, manuals and magazines	57	25	13	9
Drawing on the skills you picked up while studying for a qualification	53	26	13	9
Training courses paid for by your employer or yourself	53	21	14	12
Using skills and abilities acquired elsewhere	52	29	12	7
Using the Internet	44	20	25	12
Learning as participation				
Being shown by others how to do activities or tasks	64	22	9	6
Undertaking an activity on a regular basis	60	23	10	7
Watching and listening to others while they carry out activities	57	26	11	6
Reflecting on your performance	49	31	13	7
Using trial and error	46	30	17	7

Base: all respondents (4,932)

While a comparison of the 2007 data on improving performance at work reveals some similar patterns to the 2008 data on learning outside of the workplace, there are also a number of notable differences (see Table 2).

Undertaking a task on a regular basis is reported to be a much more helpful strategy for developing skills in the workplace (82 per cent) than for developing knowledge and skills outside of work (60 per cent). Using trial and error and reflecting on performance were also found to be more effective as workplace learning strategies.

In contrast, a number of activities categorised as learning as acquisition, such as reading books/manuals/magazines, using the internet, and using skills and abilities acquired elsewhere are cited by a greater proportion of respondents as being 'very or quite helpful' in developing knowledge and skills outside of work.

Table 2: Forms of learning and skills development found to be 'very or quite helpful' – In, and outside of, the workplace compared

Learning and skills development outside of work 2008		Improving job performance at work 2007	
Learning as acquisition	**%**		**%**
Reading books, manuals and magazines	57	Reading books, manuals and work-related magazines	39
Training courses paid for by your employer or yourself	53	Training courses paid for by your employer or yourself	54
Drawing on the skills you picked up while studying for a qualification	53	Drawing on the skills you picked up while studying for a qualification	45
Using skills and abilities acquired elsewhere	52	Using skills and abilities acquired outside of work	42
Using the Internet	44	Using the Internet	29
Learning as participation			
Being shown by others how to do activities or tasks	64	Being shown by others how to do activities or tasks	62
Undertaking an activity on a regular basis	60	Doing your job on a regular basis	82
Watching and listening to others while they carry out activities	57	Watching and listening to others while they carry out their work	56
Reflecting on your performance	49	Reflecting on your performance	53
Using trial and error	46	Using trial and error on the job	53
Weighted base: all respondents	4,932	Weighted base: all employees	2,076

Learning and skills development – analysis by learning status and future intentions to learn

Respondents who have participated in learning during the previous three years are more likely to say that they have found each of the forms of learning to be very or quite helpful in developing their knowledge and skills outside of the workplace, than those who have not participated in learning since leaving full-time education or those whose participation took place more than three years ago (see Table 3).

This decline in helpfulness by learning status is particularly apparent in relation to using the internet, drawing on skills picked up while studying for a qualification and reflecting on performance, while for other forms of learning the decline is less steep.

Being shown by others how to do activities or tasks (54 per cent), undertaking an activity on a regular basis (48 per cent) and watching and listening to others while they carry out activities (48 per cent) – all forms of learning as participation – are considered to be very or quite helpful by around one-half of respondents who have not participated in learning since leaving full-time education. A similar proportion of respondents in this category (47 per cent) also cite reading books, manuals and magazines as being helpful.

Table 3: Forms of learning and skills development found to be 'very or quite helpful' outside of work, by learning status

	Total %	Current learners %	Recent learners[a] %	Past learners[b] %	Not since leaving full-time education %
Learning as acquisition					
Reading books, manuals and magazines	57	66	64	59	47
Training courses paid for by your employer or yourself	53	62	64	55	41
Drawing on the skills you picked up while studying for a qualification	53	73	65	53	37
Using skills and abilities acquired elsewhere	52	65	60	55	40
Using the Internet	44	64	53	42	30
Learning as participation					
Being shown by others how to do activities or tasks	64	70	73	67	54
Undertaking an activity on a regular basis	60	71	69	61	48
Watching and listening to others while they carry out activities	57	65	65	59	48
Reflecting on your performance	49	63	55	49	38
Using trial and error	46	52	49	49	41
Weighted base	4,932	965	932	1,278	1,687

Base: all respondents

a. In the last three years
b. More thann three years ago

In a similar way, respondents who say that they intend to take up learning in the next three years are also more likely to report finding each of the forms of learning to be helpful in developing their knowledge and skills, than those who say that they are unlikely to learn in the future (see Table 4).

Even among those respondents who say that they are unlikely to participate in learning in the next three years, the proportions that find each of these strategies for learning helpful in developing their knowledge and skills are not small. This may suggest either that these respondents do not identify their strategies for developing knowledge and skills as 'learning', or that whilst they do not anticipate the need to develop knowledge and skills, they are confident that they would have the tools to hand should they do so.

Table 4: Forms of learning and skills development found to be 'very or quite helpful' outside of work, by future intentions to learn

	Likely to learn %	Not likely to learn %
Learning as acquisition		
Reading books, manuals and magazines	65	52
Training courses paid for by your employer or yourself	65	47
Drawing on the skills you picked up while studying for a qualification	66	45
Using skills and abilities acquired elsewhere	61	47
Using the Internet	58	34
Learning as participation		
Being shown by others how to do activities or tasks	72	60
Undertaking an activity on a regular basis	70	53
Watching and listening to others while they carry out activities	66	52
Reflecting on your performance	58	42
Using trial and error	52	43
Weighted base	965	932

Base: all respondents not in full-time education

Learning and skills development – analysis by gender

Analysis by gender shows that, with the exception of reading books, magazines and manuals and using the Internet, men are more likely than women to consider each of these forms of learning to be helpful in developing knowledge and skills outside of the workplace. In general, however, these differences are small, with only those in relation to training courses, using skills and abilities acquired elsewhere and using trial and error being statistically significant (see Table 5).

These figures contrast with those found in 2007 when the survey looked at the helpfulness of each of these forms of learning in improving job performance. The 2007 data showed that with the exception of reading books, manuals and magazines, women were more likely than men to rate all forms of learning as being very or quite helpful.

Table 5: Forms of learning and skills development found to be 'very or quite helpful' outside of work, by gender

	Total %	Men %	Women %
Learning as acquisition			
Reading books, manuals and magazines	57	56	58
Training courses paid for by your employer or yourself	53	56	50
Drawing on the skills you picked up while studying for a qualification	53	54	52
Using skills and abilities acquired elsewhere	52	55	50
Using the Internet	44	44	44
Learning as participation			
Being shown by others how to do activities or tasks	64	64	63
Undertaking an activity on a regular basis	60	61	59
Watching and listening to others while they carry out activities	57	58	56
Reflecting on your performance	49	50	47
Using trial and error	46	49	44
Weighted base	4,932	2,396	2,537

Base: all respondents

Learning and skills development – analysis by socio-economic class

In general, the proportion of respondents who say that they have found any of these forms of learning helpful in developing their skills and knowledge outside of work is greater in higher socio-economic classes,[7] with differences between higher and lower classes tending to be greater among activities classified as learning as acquisition (see Table 6).

With the exception of training courses, the decline in helpfulness of forms of 'learning as acquisition' across socio-economic classes, is much less evident in this years survey, than that found in the 2007 survey which focused on forms of learning that improve job performance. For example in 2007, twice as many ABs (54 per cent) said that they found the skills picked up while studying for a qualification to be very or quite helpful in improving their performance at work, compared with DEs (27 per cent). In 2008, 64 per cent of ABs cited this form of learning as helpful in developing knowledge and skills outside of work, as did 43 per cent of DEs.

In contrast, there is a much more steep decline in helpfulness across socio-economic classes for most forms of 'learning as participation', in 2008 than found in the 2007 survey.

Table 6: Forms of learning and skills development found to be 'very or quite helpful' outside of work, by socio-economic class

	Total %	AB %	C1 %	C2 %	DE %
Learning as acquisition					
Reading books, manuals and magazines	57	66	60	53	49
Training courses paid for by your employer or yourself	53	60	59	54	42
Drawing on the skills you picked up while studying for a qualification	53	64	57	50	43
Using skills and abilities acquired elsewhere	52	59	56	51	45
Using the Internet	44	55	52	41	32
Learning as participation					
Being shown by others how to do activities or tasks	64	71	68	59	50
Undertaking an activity on a regular basis	60	69	63	59	50
Watching and listening to others while they carry out activities	57	63	61	55	51
Reflecting on your performance	49	57	52	47	41
Using trial and error	46	48	48	48	42
Weighted base	4,932	992	1,454	1,017	1,469

Base: all respondents

7 Social Grade A includes the upper and upper-middle classes and is generally grouped with Grade B, the middle classes. Grade C1 includes the lower-middle class, often called white-collar workers. Grade C2 mainly consists of skilled manual workers. Grade D comprises the semi-skilled and unskilled working class, and is usually linked with Grade E, those on the lowest levels of subsistence such as old age pensioners and those dependent upon welfare benefits.

Learning and skills development – analysis by employment status

Respondents in employment, or who are registered as unemployed, are generally more likely to cite each of the forms of learning as being helpful in developing their knowledge and skills outside of work, than respondents who are not working, or who are retired (see Table 7).

As with the 2007 survey on improving job performance, full-time workers are more likely than those working part time to find most sources of learning helpful in developing knowledge and skills

Being shown by others how to do activities or tasks is rated as being the most helpful form of learning by respondents across all categories of employment status, although among retired adults, developing knowledge and skills through reading books, manuals and magazines is equally as important. Retired respondents are, however, much less likely to cite using the Internet as a helpful form of learning then respondents of other employment status.

Table 7: Forms of learning and skills development found to be 'very or quite helpful' outside of work, by employment status

	Total %	Full time %	Part time %	Unemployed[a] %	Not working %	Retired %
Learning as acquisition						
Reading books, manuals and magazines	57	57	57	59	55	55
Training courses paid for by your employer or yourself	53	61	56	58	48	41
Drawing on the skills you picked up while studying for a qualification	53	57	56	57	49	44
Using skills and abilities acquired elsewhere	52	57	51	57	51	44
Using the Internet	44	54	49	56	41	22
Learning as participation						
Being shown by others how to do activities or tasks	64	69	65	67	62	55
Undertaking an activity on a regular basis	60	64	60	64	58	52
Watching and listening to others while they carry out activities	57	62	59	59	55	49
Reflecting on your performance	49	53	50	53	41	42
Using trial and error	46	51	45	45	46	40
Weighted base	4,932	992	1,454	1,017	1,469	1,275

Base: all respondents

a. Includes only those who are registered as unemployed and claiming JSA.

Learning and skills development – analysis by age

In general, older adults tend to find most forms of learning less helpful in developing their knowledge and skills outside of the workplace, than younger adults (see Table 8). Younger adults, in particular, value being shown by others how to do activities or tasks, while learning from training courses, using skills and abilities acquired elsewhere and learning through trial and error are thought to be particularly helpful by adults in their thirties.

The helpfulness of learning through reading books, manuals and magazines is most consistent across age groups, with the most significant decline being in relation to use of the Internet.

Table 8: Forms of learning and skills development found to be 'very or quite helpful' outside of work, by terminal age of education

	Total %	17–24 %	25–34 %	35–44 %	45–54 %	55–64 %	65–74 %	75+ %
Learning as acquisition								
Reading books, manuals and magazines	57	55	59	59	55	59	54	53
Training courses paid for by your employer or yourself	53	57	63	59	52	53	43	33
Drawing on the skills you picked up while studying for a qualification	53	61	59	57	51	53	45	37
Using skills and abilities acquired elsewhere	52	58	54	58	51	51	44	41
Using the Internet	44	62	59	55	42	37	21	14
Learning as participation								
Being shown by others how to do activities or tasks	64	70	68	70	63	61	57	49
Undertaking an activity on a regular basis	60	67	65	65	58	57	53	44
Watching and listening to others while they carry out activities	57	61	64	62	56	54	50	46
Reflecting on your performance	49	53	54	52	47	46	43	37
Using trial and error	46	49	53	49	44	45	41	36
Weighted base	4,932	637	803	954	761	808	545	423

Base: all respondents

Learning and skills development – analysis by terminal age of education

Those who stay on at school, even for a short while, are more likely then those who leave at the earliest opportunity to say that most forms of learning are very or quite helpful in developing knowledge and skills outside of work. The exception to this is in relation to using trial and error, where similar proportions of respondents in each category report finding this helpful (see Table 9).

Those who left full-stime education aged 19-20, identify learning through attendance on a training course as being the second most helpful form of learning in which they have been engaged. For other groups of adults, this form of learning is relatively less important.

Table 9: Forms of learning and skills development found to be 'very or quite helpful' outside of work, by terminal age of education

	Total %	Up to 16 %	17-18 %	19-20 %	21+ %
Learning as acquisition					
Reading books, manuals and magazines	57	53	58	58	66
Training courses paid for by your employer or yourself	53	48	58	60	63
Drawing on the skills you picked up while studying for a qualification	53	46	57	55	66
Using skills and abilities acquired elsewhere	52	47	56	57	61
Using the Internet	44	33	51	54	61
Learning as participation					
Being shown by others how to do activities or tasks	64	61	68	66	69
Undertaking an activity on a regular basis	60	55	65	58	69
Watching and listening to others while they carry out activities	57	55	59	59	64
Reflecting on your performance	49	44	48	54	58
Using trial and error	46	47	46	45	45
Weighted base	4,932	992	1,454	1,017	1,469

Base: all respondents